12.1.04

www.NASH-???.com

DIAMONDS IN THE ROUGH

To Mike

With cool people like you, we need more beer + vacations

Peace out
NASH

Diamonds in the Rough

THE YOUTH OF AMERICA

By

Nash Hasan

PORTLAND • OREGON
INKWATERPRESS.COM

Acknowledgments

I do appreciate Inkwater Press's philosophy and approach in publishing their books. Not only did they make it possible for me to publish my first book, they also provided me with much needed guidance and support through out the development, writing, editing, designing, and production phases. I do appreciate their patience with me throughout this process, as well.

Acknowledgment is hereby extended to all those who opened their hearts and shared their life stories with me over the past four years. I do miss you all and wish you well in your future endeavors.

Copyright © 2007 by Nash Hasan

Cover and interior design by Masha Shubin
Author's photos by: Marie Saturn, Saturn Style Studios
    Cover Photo: Shadowed bodyscape © 2007 Valentin Casarsa.
    Just Dark: Spooky Grave © 2005 Auke Holwerda
    Dusk: I Was Here © 2007 Bonnie Schupp .
    Twilight: When Angels Cry #2 © 2006 Lev Dolgachov.
    Dawn: Bright Future © 2007 Peter Miller
    Bright Light: Into the World © 2005 Joshua Blake.
    Images from iStockPhoto.com

All rights reserved. No part of this book may be reproduced or transmitted in any form or by any means whatsoever, including photocopying, recording or by any information storage and retrieval system, without written permission from the publisher and/or author. Contact Inkwater Press at 6750 SW Franklin Street, Suite A, Portland, OR 97223-2542. 503.968.6777

www.inkwaterpress.com

ISBN-13 978-1-59299-300-0
ISBN-10 1-59299-300-1

Publisher: Inkwater Press

Printed in the U.S.A.
All paper is acid free and meets all ANSI standards for archival quality paper.

Dedicated
To

Mom & Dad, Sisters & Brother, the Bullock family,
Dr. Inman's family, Grandma Shaw; the Castle family,
and all those who opened their hearts, shared their
stories, and inspired me to write this book.

Contents

Just Dark 1

Dusk 27

Twilight 61

Dawn 95

Bright Light 125

Introduction

I began writing the words of young women and men's silent cries four years ago. Some of them had nurturing and loving parents—others didn't. Some of them came from broken homes. Others wished they weren't born. Many were lonely, but not alone in the world of lonely.

DAWN estimates, out of the 132,582 Emergency Department (ED) visits for drug-related suicide attempts in 2005, people 12–24 years of age accounted for 44,168 visits.[1]

Saddened by their tragedies, humbled by their humility and intrigued by their talents and personalities, I decided to reach out to them, and began quickly immersing myself into many aspects of their lives.

Since 2003, I visited, and informally interviewed hundreds of people, offered them assistance and opened my home to the ones who were in dire need for a temporary place to stay.

At midyear 2006, approximately 475,800 out of 2,245,000 inmates in the custody of State and Federal prisons and local jails are 18-24 years of age.[2]

In January 2004, after I had a narrow escape from death, I felt compelled to write and convey their stories. Therefore, in October 2006, I resigned from my previous career in Facilities and Construction Management, stopped conducting any further Management – Leadership training programs, and began dedicating my time and energy fully toward writing this book. My hopes for this work are:

<u>First,</u> increasing society's awareness of the magnitude and seriousness of the issues on hand
<u>Second,</u> encouraging the youth to voice and bring their problems into the open

---

[1] DAWN (Drug Abuse Warning Network), 2005: National Estimates of Drug-Related, Emergency Department Visits U.S. DEPARTMENT OF HEALTH AND HUMAN SERVICES Substance Abuse and Mental Health Services Administration, Feb 2007
[2] Bureau of Justice Statistics Bulletin June 207, NCJ 217675

<u>Third,</u> inspiring the youth to take charge of their lives.

"A poem is energy transferred from where the poet got it...by way of the poem itself to, all the way over to, the reader."[3] Charles Olson

The book consists of 40 poems, divided equally into five chapters. The chapters' titles are named in degrees of sunlight (and) relative to a certain period of the day, beginning with grim and dark poems relating to sexual abuse and suicide, and ending with inspiring and uplifting poems such as "Hope" and "Future Dreams."

Today, the forces shaping children's nurturing environment are much more complex than ever before. Internet access and use, media advertising and programming, among many others, play a significant role in the development and behavior of children. We can no longer attribute the problems of our youth today, solely, on the break-up of the "Two-Parent" family unit.

"In 2004, admissions of young adults—those aged 18 to 25—accounted for almost 390,000 of the approximately 1.9 million annual admissions to substance treatment facilities in the Treatment Episode Data Set (TEDS)."[4]

Prior to locking up more of our troubled youth and/or writing them off as mentally ill, we ought to look into the environment we provided for them as they were growing up. We must come up with alternate solutions to the problems we have on hand. After all, jails and prisons won't fix everyone nor provide a better nurturing environment for the children of tomorrow.

In conclusion, most of our youth, today, are in dire need of our attention and not detention, our encouragement and not punishment, and most of all, they are in need of people who will believe in them and not walk away.

---

[3] Quote of the day MSN.Com September 26, 2005
[4] The DASIS Report issue 21 (2006) by the Office of Applied Studies, Substance Abuse and Mental Health Services Administration (SAMHSA). www.samhsa.gov

Just Dark

Yesterday, You Promised 3
In Your Names 4
How Much Can I Take 7
Scream 9
A Felon on the Run 13
Hurting 19
Missing Their Teens 21
Held Hostage without Freewill 23

Yesterday, You Promised

Yesterday,
You promised me your soul
Today,
You don't bother,
Answering my calls

Yesterday,
Your words gave me life
Today,
Your words slay me like a knife

Yesterday,
You meant the world to me
Today, without you,
My world is empty

Yesterday, you said
You'd be there for me forever and ever
Today, I know
Never to believe you, never ever

What happened
Was I, just
A figment of your imagination
Or,
You just have discovered
I'm not worthy of your love

In Your Names

I write, "In Your Names"
To help ease the pain
Of the ones left behind
Lonely and without
Anyone to claim
As family of the same
Blood running
Through their veins

Innocent children
Deprived of affection
Longing for attention
Lost to addictions
Sinking into depression
Victims living
Lives to recon
The beginning,
Of their ending

Overdosed and died
Committed suicide
Or gunned down
To the ground

Marked remains
Of their bloodstains
Washed down
Curbside street drains
Slain in vain
Nothing to gain
Many to blame
Much to learn

Sadly, insane
Seeing it repeated
Again and again
Lame,
Televising their names
"Breaking News" stories
Glorified for glory
Dramatized for ratings
Short blips in between
Commercials previously seen
On TV's flat screens

Screaming to convey
Of a tragedy
Quickly spreading
Across the country

Aiming for,
An easy prey
In millions of youth,
Living today
Many of whom,
Grew up in disarray
Since their parents,
Died or went away

Traumatized in fear
Running with their peers
Traveling the trails
Leading them astray
To their short-lived fate

Children trampled
Adults in shambles
Willing to gamble
Their conscience away

Sold their morals
For cheap commercials
Clinging on clichés
Of media campaigns
For political gains

Voting in dismay
For new lousy laws
Targeting,
Their own children
Sending them away
Serving time
Behind bars,
For adolescent crimes

Hoping for discipline
Naïve,
Only discovering
Hardened criminals
Hunted down,
As felons
Locked up behind,
In prisons
Till they're finally found
Broken,
Into ruins

Isn't time,
To listen
To what your children,
Have to say
If it's not now,
Then when?

p.s. In Memory of Cody, Ivy, and Nate

How Much Can I Take

"How much can I take?"
"How much can I take?"
God help me
"How much can I take?"

Born,
Three months prematurely
What's the fucking rush?
I couldn't breathe
On my own

I didn't have the dignity
Of clean sheets
In a hospital bed
Wrapped up in a blanket
In a dark alley,
She found me,
She said

At two,
Mommy said,
"Baby, I must go,
You'll be all alone"

At sixteen,
Daddy said,
"It's time to go,
You're on your own"

At fourteen,
I had my first abortion
I didn't know then

What love was all about
At twenty,
I had another one
Not till then,
That I knew
What love
Is all about

It's about
Someone
Physically raping me,
Emotionally draining me,
And
Mentally abusing me

"How much can I take?"
Were not her words
They were my words of her
While she was,
Crying on my shoulder
Hunting for an advice
Helping her heal
The injured soul
Terrorizing her life
The one who tells her
"I love you"

Remember, what
"Love"
Means to her

Scream

Hey Mister
Excuse Ma'am
Hey you, over there
I'm begging you
Please,
Don't walk away
And leave me alone
In my own
Misery and fear

Can you
Spare me a dime
A quarter,
Or, just buy me a beer

What's my body
Worth to you, my dear
I promise you
I'll do anything you want
And I'll disappear

I am hungry
I am cold
Wish the end were so near

Can't you understand me
Choosing to be
Living on the streets?
Running away from home
To escape the ugly treats

Night after night
Awaiting his arrival
In panic and fear
Crying,
For someone's help
To rid me of
The Monster Queer

Closing my eyes
Not wanting to see
Numbing my brain
Not wanting to feel
His dirty hands
Crawling all over me

Groping my breast
Getting me undressed
Whispering in my ears
Leaving me behind
Traumatized
With haunting dreams

Can't anyone
Hear me "Scream"?
Can't you see,
My cries,
And agonizing tears

A child growing up
On hate and anger
With tormenting guilt
For so many years

Resigned,
Into thinking
I was,
The deserving freak

Fucked up on drugs
To escape
The ugliness
Of what was
Becoming so real

Slashing my wrists
To escape his pain
Wanting to die
Before he could hurt me, again

Living his lies
Not letting it out
Fearing for my life
Should he ever find out

Screaming,
Crying
Fighting
Keeping it inside
Deep down and concealed
Where no one can discover

Running away
From "Hell"
To the streets
Hiding
Under cover

To save
My sanity,
My soul,
My life,
If you care
To understand me better

Hoping
Someday,
Somewhere,
Somehow,
I can recover

A Felon on the Run

"Flight Risk"
An inmate
In a bulletproof vest
Refusing to consent
Determined to contest
All the charges and arrest

Traveling,
Night by night
Underneath,
The stars and moon light

Bound,
By no laws of the land
Maneuvering,
Stealth without a sound

Camouflaged,
In blue jeans and a baseball cap
Helping him,
Appear and disappear,
Quickly into the crowds

Entertaining,
At people's gatherings
In small towns and camp grounds

Singing them songs
Of a young man
He met along
His traveling

Appearing,
Innocent and calm
Not posing any harm
Yet, seemingly wary
Of anyone
Befriended him

Many of those he trusted
Were informants lying
Trying to rob him
Before he gets busted

"A Felon on the Run"
Trusting of no one
Polite and bright
Despite,
His cold hardened heart

Tiny built and small
Yet, mighty
Ruthless in a brawl

Hungry and lean
A runaway teen
Breaking into
Vending machines
For candy to eat
And coins to keep

A rocky start at thirteen
A savvy hustler by sixteen
He made lots of money
But, lost it
Quickly in a hurry
As he began
Falling into

Vicious cycles
Of crimes and fines
Hardly worth
Him serving time

Skipping his hearings
Neglecting court sentencing
Violating parole instructions
Getting caught with possession
Not giving a damn
About anything
Cause,
Already, he had lost
Everything

Surrendering
To suicidal thoughts
Trusting,
There was no way out
Crying out loud
"What the fuck is it all about?"
Nobody,
Gave a damn
About my sorry ass
As a homeless child
In Burbank
Or living
On the streets
Of Portland's
Felony Flats

Many inmates,
In jails or prisons
Or out
On the streets, living
Became,
Convicted felons
Before
They were twenty-one

Born bruised
Raised abused
Grew up confused
Addicted to
Drugs and booze
Ended up
Making the "News"
As convicts of no use

Addressing the problems
Of felons and felonies
By the voting majority
Is a sign of insanity

The dilemma
In reality
To the formula
Of morality
Is lacking
Parental liability
And societal
Accountability

Creating,
Tougher laws for crimes
Adding more jail cells for time
Is, in itself
A despicable crime

Building more jail space
Instead of,
Schools in the first place
Is a disgrace
To the human race

All talks and laws
Jail cells and walls
Won't fix
A damn thing at all

The failure of one
Is the failure of many

Ending his story
With,
A sad tone in his voice
Saying it
With,
A sigh of relief

I am an outlaw,
Not a felon
I am a drug user,
Not a murderer
I am a victim,
Not a criminal

It has been a long time coming
For the showdown to begin
In hunting me down
With K9 officers and guns
I'm tired of being on the run
I am done

Hurting

The incredible sound
Of your enchanting voice
Singing the words
Of a heart-felt song
With rhythm and soul
Telling them all
I'm "Hurting"

Screaming it loud
Reciting it to the crowd
Uncertain,
If anyone
Is listening

Giving in
To your haunting doubts
Living in
Your fictitious thoughts

Tripping out on treats
Depriving you of sleep
Destroying your systems
Without your permission

Surrendering,
Your existence
Without any,
Resistance

Too weakened to fight
The disease of addiction
The anxiety and depression

You gave up on living
Early from the beginning
Now, you're wondering
If there is peace in ending
Life before its timing

Falling too deep
Into selfish deeds
Bound to bleed
Beyond
Your will to heal

"Hurting" bad
Confound
To the ground
Unable to rebound

All alone
On your own
No sound
No crowd
No one around

Missing Their Teens

Darkened clouds
Thundering loud
Hurricanes and winds
Blowing to no end
Mountains flattened
Animals frightened
Distraught crowds
Wearing shrouds

Praying and mourning
For mercy and affection
To be descending
Upon all
Abandoned children

Born deprived
Compassion denied
Poorly treated
Used and defeated

Attending to their siblings
While Mommy and Daddy serve
Time for their crime

Lonely and frightened
Mounting hatred
Hearts darkened
Silently crying
Slowly dying
Hiding in fear
Dried up of tears

Roaming the streets
For tricks and treats
Searching for a place to sleep
Begging for something to eat

Raised by their peers
"Missing Their Teens"
Grew up repeating
All they were resenting
As they are rearing
Their own offspring

A vicious cycle to no end
A dark story, I'm telling
Stop dodging it and running
Responsibility to be taken
Don't be mistaken
It is time to be awakened
Now, and not then
Today, and not when

Held Hostage without Freewill

A Powerful enemy
Known for debauchery
Ruthless and mighty
Maneuvering
Stealthily and swiftly
Crossing all boundaries of society
Embracing diversity
Accepting of all ethnicities
Promoting gender equality
Recruiting indiscriminately
The young and elderly
The poor and wealthy
The ill and healthy
Prescribed medically
For trauma and surgery
Mental health and anxiety
The cure for all and any
Alluring all, with many
Illusions and fantasies
Of sex, drugs and money

An open invitation to the party
As an honorary guest or as royalty
Come on in, celebrate, and be merry
Lots of "party favors" on hand
Tempted, but you hold off for a while
Sooner or later,
You surrender and give it a try
A casual user
Who took it once in a while
Became an addict
Wanting it all the time

Needing it to chill out and be happy
Or, just to boost your energy
Thinking you could walk away
In denial,
It's addiction you defy
You can't get it out of your mind
You are a hostage to its "All-Mighty"
The mighty enemy
A mercenary without mercy
Bound by no boundaries
Aims to hypnotize many
Leading them astray
To robbery and adultery
Of their friends and family

All surrendered in solidarity
To be confined, in solitary
To a dark bottomless hole
Difficult to get out of on your own
Some won't make it out at all
Overdosed and died
Or, committed suicide
Burned to ashes
Or buried 6 feet under ground
The enemy has already
Written your obituary

"Held Hostage without Freewill"
You became a slave at his will
Giving it up all in a hurry
Including your job and money
Crying, you want to die
Lying, you just want to be
Fucked up and high

Higher and higher
Never satisfied
Wanting stronger shit to try
Crystal or ecstasy
A ball of crack or just a "T"
Acid or 'shrooms
Vicodin or heroin
Snorting or inhaling
Shooting or smoking
Through your nose or your vein
It all ends the same
Clueless, you don't know a thing

Many will come to your rescue
Wishing they, only, knew
You had no intentions
In coming through
These words won't help you
Nor, will they save you
They'll have no bearing on you
Surrender your free will if you will
Your story will be too short to tell
As you and I know how it'll end
"The End"

Dusk

Dear Isaac 29
Hope and Hannah 34
Scarlet & Alabama 38
Enabling You to Stay the Same 43
Her 47
Not Worth the Fight 50
Don - till Dusk 52
Goodbye, My Friend 57

Dear Isaac

Capturing the words
Still ringing in my ears
Of your mother's voice
Crying in fear
While watching
The tears
Crawling down
Her cheeks
Releasing,
Pent-up emotions
Defusing,
Built-up tensions

Guiltily stating,
She hasn't been around
As a good mother
Should have

Missing,
Your essence
Longing,
For your presence

Saddened,
For the hours disappearing
Without you being near her

She had been working
The early hours of the evening
Till
The early hours of the morning

Entertaining the crowds
Baring it all loud

An exotic stripper
With pizzazz
An erotic dancer
With all that Jazz

Living, polarized,
In-between,
Her family life
And the night life

Galvanized,
To endure
Like no one I knew
At the age
Of twenty-two

She was a young gal
From a small town
Just outside
Spokane, Washington

She had moved out,
On her own
Many miles,
Away from home
Just, shortly,
After you're born

Leaving behind
Many of her memories
As a child

She'd been in love
With the man of her dreams
Since her early Sophomore year

She was a teen idol at school
With grand plans to pursue
College classes and tuitions
Decent jobs and traveling
Honeymoon and a wedding
Till it all came down crashing
On her day of graduation

Discovering,
She'd been pregnant with a child
Since that very special Prom Night
It was the night,
Without a doubt
That changed her life,
Forever after that
With liquor and wine,
Going down
Smoking weed,
Soaking deep
Into their veins,
Quickly,
To their brains
Lovemaking,
Was insane

Euphoric and excited
Saddened and frightened
Till he decided
He wanted nothing to do with it
Leaving her behind
Saddened and traumatized

Despite,
Her religious beliefs
The counseling
And the grief
She decided
She was keeping her baby
Regardless of
The price to pay
Or
The sacrifice to make
Abortion, was not an option
Adoption, was out of the question

A single Mommy
Raising her baby
A teenager,
Gone wild and crazy
Traveling
Small towns and big cities
Baring it all out
Quickly and in a hurry
Earning the dollars
Helping her pay
For rent and baby sitters

A pretty woman
Adored by many
Lawyers and bankers
Bikers and gangsters
Claiming to be
Friends and lovers
While alluring her
With downers and uppers

And breaking her heart
Onetime after another

"Dear Isaac"
You ought to remember
Many people,
With handicapped bodies,
Do not have handicapped souls
While, some others
Without handicapped bodies
Do have handicapped souls
Pray for those ones

Your Mom
Was just a teenage mother
Though,
It didn't take her
Much to discover
How the world around her
Could change in an hour
Frequent and forever

I, still do remember
Seeing her teary eyes
Wearing her smile
And saying
"Soon, he'll be three"

It has been years
Since,
I saw her last
I wish you two
The very best
From my heart

Sincerely Yours

Hope and Hannah

I wrote you the letters
Returned, undelivered
I made the countless calls
Disappointed,
No one answered at all
I fought
For my visitation rights
Denied ,
Each time, I tried

I prayed to the God above
I grieved to the ones I love
I chanted to the winds
I cried to many of my friends

I called on
The flocks of birds
Migrating North and South
If they'd deliver these words
Into the hands
Of the most beautiful girls
In my world,
"Hope and Hannah"

Wanting you to know,
Despite,
The years that passed us by
The distance splitting us apart
The time it may take us till we reunite
You'll always be on my mind
And you'll always have
A sacred place in my heart

Girls,
Your memories,
Keep me alive
Your smiles,
Brighten my nights

My girl Hope,
Your courage helps me cope
My girl Hannah,
I find strength in your persona

I know,
It wasn't cool
Letting my problems
Get to you

I'm truly sorry
For all you went through

I do ask you
For forgiveness
As I still do
Pay the price, today
For all of the mistakes
I made, yesterday

I do regret
Missing
The once chance I had
To be
The good father
As I should have

You were toddlers, then
You are teenagers, now
Wish I were near
To help see you
Through these
Tough teen years

Soon,
Flocks of boys
Will be
Swarming around
Like vultures
Hunting for
An easy prey

Appearing cool
Acting fool

Claiming to be
Madly "In love"
Knowing well,
It isn't true

Cause,
Love
Doesn't know hurting
It only knows healing
Love
Doesn't know taking
It only knows giving
Love
Isn't about
A blackened eye
A fat lip

Or a broken nose
It's about
Healing your wound
Helping you mend
And freeing your soul

Won't you wait and see
Till you know for sure
Who is real
And, who is not

Hoping, you'll be laughing then
Rather than crying for being
Just another falling victim

God bless

Scarlet & Alabama

A teenager out of school
Loving her life and living it, too

Scarlet is her name
Dancing was her game

A "red-headed" girl,
And a "Barbie" doll
Street smart, sassy,
And a fireball
Who'd easily,
Jump into a brawl
To break up fighting,
She abhors

Driven by curiosity
She went out
Traveling to Sin City
Venturing out to explore
Las Vegas and more

Dancing for living
Survived the transition
Despite the competition

Flying out to the scenes
Tasting the town
Roaming the streets
Having some fun
Till she ran
Into the man
Of her dreams

And, ended up
Marrying him
Quickly on a whim
Bringing Alabama
To be with them

A Hound Dog she adopted
Loved and never neglected
Alabama was her family
She was Alabama's best buddy

Shortly, after the honeymoon was over
Her husband's demeanor became meaner
As he began treating her like shit
Day and night, he'd never quit

Alabama became jealous
Irritated and zealous
Though,
She kept him intact
Despite, the urge to attack
Respecting, her Mommy's demands
Obeying, her Master's commands

Till that
One unforgettable evening
Arriving home late
After missing their diner date
Drunk and broken
When he stormed in
The front door
Breaking it wide open

Catching Scarlet off guard
Sending her into shock
Shaken and alarmed
Without uttering a sound
Refusing to answer
His demeaning questions
Not fazed by
The garbage
He was spouting
Out of
His drunken ass
Of the shit he was
Most guilty of

Not daring to call
The neighbors
Nor the police
Fearing for her life
If he were to be
Booked and released

By then, Alabama
Had moved in
Growling and barking
Warning him

She's guarding her Momma
From any B.S. or drama

He tricked Alabama,
With a treat
Knocking her down,
To his feet
And began unleashing,

Countless blows
To the head
Dragging her outside
Wanting her dead

Scarlet jumped in
Kicking and screaming
Begging him to let go
Of her, only, child

Clenching his fists
And walking away
Promising them,
Without remorse
"Next time,
It'll be a lot worse"

That was the night
That sent them packing
And out of town
Without ever
Thinking
Of coming back

Scarlet was telling me
Her story and crying
Wondering,
What would've been her fate
If it wasn't for Alabama that day
Saving her life
Moreover,
Making her realize
How much of herself
She had lost and sacrificed

By then,
I couldn't help it noticing
Alabama setting
At her bedside and yawning
Pretending,
As if it were
All about nothing

Enabling You to Stay the Same

Pretending,
As if you don't know why
The reasons,
I won't be hanging around
"On stand by"
Just to watch you suffer
Till you slowly die

How many more lies
Will you tell me in disguise
Behind the tears in your eyes
And your bloody,
Cold and heartless cries

How much longer can you justify
Staying fucked up and high

Baby, I am tired of your game
It's fucking driving me insane
I know, it's lame
Leaving you behind
Wondering, each day
If you were dead or alive

What a shame
A beautiful girl
Ordained in pain
Living insane
A life of calamity
Marked for tragedy
Destined to catastrophe
Fatherless child

Raised wild
Grew up mad
Seeing mommy sad
Insulted and mistreated
Refusing it
To be repeated

Trusting in predators
For downers and uppers
Helping you mask over
The pain and agony
Of your childhood memories

An ex-boyfriend
Committing suicide
With no one around

Your first grade mate
Raped by her father
Till she was eight

Getting knocked up
At sixteen by an elder
And aborting it
In weeks, shortly thereafter
Wondering, where were
Your friends and family
The teachers and preachers
The civilians and militants
Of society
At those times
Of your darkened reality

Knowing well,
What I know today
I am afraid to say
I can't help you
In any way
My love to you,
Will only be
"Enabling You to Stay the Same"

Baby, I tried
To set you free
From the nightmares
Of your ugly past
Haunting you down
For as long as you last

Baby, I tried
To break you away
From the chains
Of your darkened trails
Trapping you down
Till you're weak and frail

Baby, I tried
To save you
From the murky waters
Of deceptions and lies
Bringing you down
To your demise

Baby,
I did give
I did grieve
I did forgive

I did forget
I did forego
And, now
I must go

Knowing,
You'll be
Trashing
My name
In vain
The day
I walk away

Needing to remember,
Though
This is just the way
The game is played
These days
No hard feelings

Her

Slender and tall
Silently strolls
To the dance floor
Encore
Glamour galore
Of heart and soul
And a booty to adore
Attempting to ignore
The night before
Living in fear
Year after year
Fed up with his lies
And being terrorized
She is dumping his ass
To get rid of her past

Lonely and sad
Tipsy and high
Innocence,
Gone wild

Hardcore
Taunting and flaunting
Her beauty and sex appeal

Sweet angel of sin
In a smooth tanned skin
Stunning eyes in sage
Striking lips in beige
Silky smooth hair
Down to her waist

Red fiery fingernails
And kick-ass heels
Ripping her clothes
Piece by piece
Revealing
Hidden piercing
Stripping to tease
Not to appease
Hunting for
A "Sugar Daddy" to pour
Dollars, gifts and more

Drinking booze
Bruised and abused
Screaming losers
Attracting abusers
Lonely and confused
She couldn't refuse
His lame excuse

Fucking with "Her" brain
Playing his dirty game
Falling for him
Again and again
Repeating
The ugly habits ingrained
Along
Her darkened trails
Trapping
Her weakened soul
Inside
Dampened walls
Of an invisible jail
From the ugly past
And for as long
As she lasts

Confessing to shame
She's deserving of pain
Begging him
For a truce
And to be brutally
Seduced
He whispered,
And nodded
She laughed,
Excited

This time
It was real
One of them
Did
Disappear

Not Worth the Fight

A thief veiled,
By the dark shadows of the night
Camouflaged as an Angel,
At the breaking dawn of sunlight

A liar, disguised
With tears in her eyes
Concealing,
Her many lies
With a soft spoken voice
In fright
Fearing, someone might
Be discovering
What she's all about

Flying, higher
Than a Kite
On uppers and downers,
Each night
Despite,
Her fear and anxiety
Of crashing down,
Into reality
After each, short-lived flight

Blessed in beauty
With magical eyes
A heavenly body
And a mesmerizing smile
Sadly concealing
The ugliness residing
Deep on the inside

Her sopping sad stories
Will break your heart
Rushing you off
To the rescue
As a "Knight in Shining Armor"
Shielding her from terror
Sheltering her from horror
Fighting her wars
Without surrendering at all
Taking chances, otherwise
You would've never have taken
For yourself or anyone else

Till you discover
You've been dishonored
Claiming, as if you were
Her "Dirty Parasite"
Despite,
The sacrifices you made in plight

Won't you let go,
Of the agony and pain
And rid yourself of the ugly "TERMITE"
This one is "Not Worth the Fight"

Don - till Dusk

I am tired
I am scared
I am about to break
I don't know, for God's sake,
How much of this shit I can take

Exhausted and beat
Not making ends need
While having to compete
With the B.S. on the street

I don't want, another, repeat
Of the same ill-treat
Getting captured and released
Traumatizing to say the least

Wondering,
If it's my fate
Inheriting,
The life I hate
Or, if it was
Just the way
I was raised
Yeah,
Childhood wasn't great
Come to think of it
I hardly remember it
But hey,
I at least
Had a place to sleep
And something to eat

Till those
Darkened years
Of my early teens
Having to endure
All I went through
Without a father near
Seeing him disappear
Without shedding a tear
Over the times
I adored
Of the memories
I thought
Would be dear
To his heart

Leaving me behind
Without remorse
Tore me up,
Of course
I guess,
It must've been
The divorce
Or, do you suppose,
It was my fault
For hanging on
Those dreams
Of my early
Childhood years?

Dawn till dusk
Took chances and risk
Hassling the streets
On my own feet
Till I was fifteen

Attempted to retreat
From living indiscreet
To the world of deceit
Denied entry
Left me behind
To a harsh society
Shaping my reality
Molding my personality
Into who
I am, today

Certain,
Of uncertainty
Just like many
Who grew up
Daydreaming
Of a ball game
With dad in the rain
Or, just coming home
To a mother who is a saint
Yeah, I made
My own share
Of mistakes
At home and school
With no one around
To set me straight
Or help me through
What I did wrong

Only, ended up
Locked up
In my room
Living in exile
Each afternoon

Yeah, it's true
It was dirty
Felt lonely
Trapped in
By sundown
But hey,
It was a room
Rent-free

I didn't mind
The lockdown
Nor roaming the streets
I just didn't care much
For living my life
In-between

Getting arrested
After
Having
Thanksgiving dinner
With my mother
Got me
Sick to my stomach
Now,
That I am locked in
I am wondering,
When will I be out again

Forgive me, please
My problems,
Aren't unique
They are,
Inherently deep
In society

Pardon me,
You ought to
Try and see
What life
Is likely to be
For someone like me
If you truly care
About the future
Of your own family

Truly Yours,
Don

Goodbye, My Friend

My friend went away
On an early Monday morning
I can't say
I didn't have
Much of a warning
He went out
Alone
In-route
To a world
I know nothing about
Leaving behind
Friends and family
And many
Of his precious memories

Saddened with dismay
Troubled needless to say
Lost and confused
In denial, I refused
Believing, it was true

The friend
I once knew
He'd be gone…………
……………. so soon

Distraught
A dream, I thought
A nightmare, no doubt
I ought to
Just, figure it all out
Searching for an answer

Refusing to surrender
Restless
Relentless
Needing to know
Why
What's up?
What's with all the hurry?
What for?
Don't you like it here anymore?
What's wrong?
Going out on your own
Without taking me along
You know
This won't be easy

You see
We used to go to D.C.
Together
It didn't matter
If it was early winter
Or late summer
I would stop by
To give him a ride
On our way out
To catch a flight
Taking us high
Up in the sky
Heading out
To the east
I promise, I tried
To be there on time
No, not this time
No, I wasn't too late
He just went out, too, early

Wishing, I'd said "Goodbye"
Crying my heart out
Tearing my soul apart

In mourning,
And, wondering
Maybe, this isn't real
Maybe, it's just a dream
Soon, he'll appear
I'll let him know,
How much I care
I'll ask him,
I'll listen to him
I'll …..

As the days went by,
In defiance, I consented
Maybe, this isn't a dream
Reluctantly, I conceded to my fears
Resigned, weakened at the knees
Realizing,
There was no sense in denying it
So, I stopped wishing
And, just, went on crying

I can still hear him laugh
I'll never forget
That look on his face
Whenever, he was about to say
"Come on now, you know better"

He was my teacher,
My friend,
And my brother

And now,
He's gone forever
I do miss him
More than ever

No, no you don't understand
There are no words
That could help me describe
How I feel

It is too late for me, now,
To say
"Goodbye, My Friend"
Goodbye
p.s. I miss you Jay

Twilight

Illusions 63
Your "Erotic Dancer" 67
Spoken Words Without Willpower 70
Isn't Time 72
Multiple Personalities 77
Words 82
There Was a Time in My Life 85
It's Time for Me to Go 90

Illusions

She was so surreal
The night
She appeared
Into my reality
On an early
April eve

I was an invitee
To her place to see
How life turned out to be
After years of misery

As she sat down
And began to reveal
Her aching memory

Tonight was his B-Day
Nate did pass away
It hasn't been a year
Since he disappeared
He died
Committed suicide
To set me free
Saddened and relieved
Drama, but no more fear

She was speaking of grief
I was frozen in disbelief
Fiction or mystery
Or, just twisted fantasy

Concealing
Behind her beauty
And sex appeal
The determination
To steal
Moving stealth
Without a squeal
Through walls
Of steel
To a place
That was sealed
And conditioned
Not to feel

Relentless, she reeled
My heart with ease
Searching for a sanctuary
For her pain and agony

We made a deal
To help each other heal
To honor, to trust
We agreed

Promises, she couldn't keep
Honor, wasn't her deed
Trust her, not to be trusted
Responsibility, doesn't apply
Respect, she'd disagree
Disrespect, for me to accept
At times, she was a saint
Yet, her reality was fake

Hoping for conclusions
To dreams and "Illusions"
Commotions and distortions
Chaos and confusion
Compromises and exclusions
It was time
For evolution
From pollution
Of delusions

An angel or a demon
Awakened or dreaming
Healing or bleeding
Faithful or cheating
Guarding or stealing
A price to be paid
Experiences to be made
Life to be changed

A suicide girl
Victim is her name
Truth brought her shame
Deception brought her fame

Blame was her strategy
Sympathy from misery
Misty tears for treats
To use and be used

An angel undiscovered
A soul that would endure
A soldier that would honor
A candle that would deliver

Light into darkness
Beauty into ugliness
Joy into sadness

Magical, to my delight
Despite,
Her warped insight
I ignored it
I tried
Thinking,
It just might
Work out

Enlightened
Without a doubt
Just hoping
I'd wake up
Tonight

Your "Erotic Dancer"

I am your "Erotic Dancer"
I am your exotic stripper
I am your "Mistress Sugar"
I am
At your service
For 24 hours
I'll give you pleasure
And, fulfill
Your heart's desire
For a donation,
If it's no bother

You can call me
"Solaria," "Star," or "Summer"
But please,
Don't treat me
Like the others
And, don't judge, too soon,
And call me a fucking sinner

I might be
Dirty in your eyes
I might be
A burden in your lives
I might be naïve
Believing,
In your promises and lies

I might be in pain,
But I won't agonize
And I might be your mistress,
But I won't apologize

For living a life
Where I have to compromise
My body and soul
For a cheap price

You come to see me daddy
For lunch, at noon
And after work
To sing me the blues
And late at night
When you're lonely, too
As I,
Bare my body and soul
To entertain you

You ask me "Baby,
"What's so new?"
While sipping
Your favorite brew,
Tipping me
A dollar or two
And watching
My curves and my moves
As I dance
To the groove

Wondering,
If you knew
That, I, absolutely,
Have no fucking clue
How to make it
In this world on my own
A runaway to the streets
From home

To escape the ugliness
I've known
Since the day
I was born

And, now,
That, I am grown
I am struggling to live
By the norm
Of a society that is so fucked up
And annoying

Night after night,
Searching for a place
That's comfortable and warm
To shelter me
Till tomorrow's dawn
I am
Your "Erotic Dancer"

Spoken Words Without Willpower

I heard the words you uttered
Of promises rarely delivered
Of words rarely honored
Of dreams easily shattered
Beginnings transpired
Inhibited by fear
Of what you may discover

Lacking the desire
To acquire
What could be better

Why do you, even, bother
Blaming others
Of what you can't deliver

Soon, it won't matter
Beginnings will expire
And end-up classified under
"Spoken Words Without Willpower"

Conditioned, to the end
Don't take a stand
Against,
Any events of your past
Leaving you behind
Trapped in a closed mind
Over the one,
That's undefined

I heard you loud
Speaking profound
Of dreams
You wish you had
Enlightened,
Without a doubt
It's just not,
What you had in mind
Always, justifying
And pretending,
You can't decide
Run and hide
And, as much as you want
Sooner, rather than later
You shall find

Few breaks are granted
Lifetime runs out,
Before getting started
Words won't matter,
When you're stranded
Tomorrow will honor
All you've acquired
As you were inspired
By your own
Spoken words with willpower

To feed the addiction
Bringing you
Anxiety and depression

Why won't you
Take a chance
For God's sake
Living the life
You've been given
Before,
You get called in
From the living

You are, only, a victim
Of your addiction
Without knowing it
No shame, in saying it
But it's insane
Denying it and hiding it
It's in your
Blood stream and veins
Your heart cells and brain
Your skin and hair

Don't let
The craving and agony
The hardship of reality
The criticism of family
The talk of society
The uncertainty and anxiety
Stand in your way
For an eternal recovery

You've got nothing
Over the ones recovering
Though, they got two
Over you

The desire,
To survive
And the willpower
To stay alive
Choosing starvation
Rather than humiliation
Bare bones
Rather than bare souls
Brave hearts
Rather than
Being strung out

Isn't time
For a new start
Tomorrow,
Doesn't care about
Your present nor your past
Tomorrow,
There won't be any timeouts
'Till you get
Your shit figured out
Tomorrow
Will be here without
Any consideration of
Your feelings or thoughts
Tomorrow
Won't be your worst enemy
Unless,
You give it the opportunity

Keep in mind
No matter
How ugly was your past
No matter
How much shit you have
No matter
How many times you've tried

Be certain,
Of the fact,
It remains

It's up to you to decide
When to turn your life around
It's up to you to decide
When to claim your life back
It's up to you to decide
When it's time for a new start

It's up to you to decide,
Whether to go after
The dreams you want
Or
The addictions you sought

Keep in mind
If there is a will, there is a way
But,
If there is no will,
There is, absolutely, no fucking way

p.s. Half-assed efforts don't count

Multiple Personalities

There are
Many of me
And I am
All of thee
Multiple
Personalities
You've seen
Of my reality
Living
In one body
Till thee
End of your time

I beg you
To stop trying
Figuring me out
You won't understand
What I am about
Others
Tried
Many times before
Till they began
Abhorring
What they were
Adoring
Bailing out
Leaving me
Behind
Trapped
In their mind
Uncertain
In doubt

Not knowing
What they found
Denying
Their discovery
Of one
Of my personalities
Residing
Within their reality

And, now
Here, you are
Trying so far
Despite
The countless calls
And the advice
From all

Madly, curious
I understand
Foolish, not
What I had
In mind

Relentless, I see
Restless, may be
Refusing to abandon
Your heart's pulse
Your soul's pull
Not fazed by
The price to pay
Nor
The sacrifice you made

You took it on
As a gambler
Stirring up
The many
Personalities
Testing
Your sanity
Without knowing
You've just begun
A journey like none
You are
A part of it now

Questioning everything
Realizing nothing
Unable to define
What your eyes see
What your ears hear
What your mind
Cannot read

Attempting,
To figure me out
Based on cognitions
Of limited definitions
To three dimensions
Of an earthly edition
I am
Yours,
Truly,

The angel sinning
The demon repenting
The light shimmering

The darkness of all
The real me
Striving to be
The unreal you
You're refusing to see
I am the heart you feel
I am the heartless you fear
I am the opposite
Of everything
I oppose nothing
I am struggling
I can't decide
Who I am
Nor whom
You want me to be

Living in
Unpredictable moods
With many
Attitudes
Of multiple personalities
Shaping my reality
Cohabitating
Within One
Earthly form
And on
Borrowed Time
With One
Precious soul
From
A heavenly source
Originating
From a pure
Intense Blue
Bright light

Born unto
This world
Discovering
Harsh struggles
Misery and troubles
Agony and pain
Till I rise, again
Evolving into
Thee healing power
For many of my
Sisters and Brothers
Traveling the universe
Living on earth
Experiencing
The many forces
Of countless powers
Consistently
Competing
Always
Opposing
One another
In one form
Or, another
Light and Dark
Love and Hate
Life and Death
Peace and War
And much more
All striving to strike a balance
In search of
A state of "Equilibrium"

Words

Words, wish you would
Help me heal the wounds
Of aching hearts
Across town and abroad
Year after year
New discoveries appear
Altering our lives and sphere
Bringing with it
Medications to cure
Our anxiety and fear
From watching
Reality shows on TV

Minute by minute
Breaking News
Dollars and cents
Weather and sport events
Broadcasting
"Live Wars" as they appear
To help us celebrate and cheer
Smart weapons with live cams
Hitting their targets on time
Blowing up bridges and dams
Innocent lives vaporized
Just like movies
We play and rewind
Followed by
Analysis and opinions
To heighten hatred and tension
Serving their intentions
Creating reality from fiction
Masters of deception

As in "Weapons of Mass Destruction"
Rushing through sanctions
Going into action
Launching wars of destruction
Unto cultures and religions
Serving their disguised missions
Of darkened visions
With assets in the black
Of stolen oil and land
And liabilities in red
Of children's blood being spilled
Depreciating the life of a foreign child
Devaluating Americans' values abroad

Board members pleased
Stockholders asleep
Demand and supply
Profits and bottom lines
Compassion denied
Political correctness re-defined
Buzzwords embraced
Short-lived and replaced
What a disgrace
To the human race
Preaching messages of civics
While breaching morality and ethics
Family members
Abandoning one another
Children running
To the streets for cover
Growing older
Tougher and bolder
Playing "Hearts," becoming popular
"Just in Time," isn't a blunder

You can rent friends by the hour
For your use as you desire
And dispose of them whenever
No one will bother,
If anyone is left behind
Bleeding along the trail
To the journey of nowhere

While the many men in power
The claimed leaders of the world
Are silenced without an utter
Ignoring mourning and crying mothers
Seeing their children die and suffer
For the "Market Value" of the "Dollar"
At the expense of million others

No sane mother would ever
Hope for pain to the child of another
Regardless of nationality or culture
Religion or skin color

A message to be delivered
Not in wars
But in words

There Was a Time in My Life

When I ran into Mom's arms
To shelter me from danger and harm
Embracing me to her chest
Telling me, I was the best
Laughing with me silly
Distracting me,
From all worries
Listening to the beats of her heart
While watching the tears in her eyes
As she was daydreaming
Of the moment in time
When I would be gone
Knowing well,
It won't be too long
Before the time comes along
For our goodbyes

There was a time in my life
When we made Dad proud
As we kissed his hand
In respect with pride
Appreciating his dedication
For working the long hours
Risking his life
Around oil wells and fires
A mission he ventured
From a vision he rendered
For us to remember
As we went out discover
The purpose of this life of ours

There was a time in my life
When we loved our neighbors
Took care of our elders
Rushed to save a toddler
We were all in it, together
We played sports
And sang songs
Broke things,
Knowing, well,
We're wrong
We paid the price
For our mistakes, twice
We laughed
More than cried
Took chances and tried
Some were, really, dumb
Like crossing busy streets
With fast moving cars
Daring the drivers
In making it
To the other side
Waking up in the ER
To my mother's cry
It wasn't funny then,
I'm lucky, I'm still alive

There was a time in my life
When our schools
Were sacred grounds
Praised to dare
Allowed us to learn
We cheated and got caught
Got grounded and rewarded
Mistakes were allowed

Neglect was denied
We respected our teachers
Despite their demeanors
We paid attention
To all the cool things
We're still remembering

There was a time in my life
When I wanted to be a pilot
Flying jet fighters in the skies
Thinking I'd be lucky to be alive
By the time I was twenty-five
Wanting to fight the wars
To bring justice to us all
Many died since then
Wars still going on
Enemies became friends
And friends became enemies
All fighting for
The soil of the Holy Land
Or the oil in Baghdad
Knowing well
No one owns
The oil nor the land
All of us were born
All of us will be gone
The oil and the land
Were there before
And will be there
Many years more
Hoping someone soon
Can figure this shit out
Before, thousands more die
Leaving

Their mothers cry
And the grandchildren
Of "Abraham,"
Asking "WHY?"

There was a time in my life
When time
Was moving slow
We wanted to get older
To stay outside longer
We went out
Venturing into the world
Aggressive and bold
With visions and dreams
Many of which, became real
We had homes and automobiles
Saving accounts without loans
Great jobs with awesome incomes
Living on the run
Having fun
Till the news
Of wars began to creep
And many of our friends
Began to leave
Fearing discrimination
And rampant hysteria
Manufactured by
Talk show hosts
And self serving media

Time started
To run out on us faster
Not for the better
We just got busier

As we began,
Filling our schedules
With many things,
Not significant

We got lots of junk mail and letters
From bankers and creditors
Mandating of us
To work the 24x7 hours
To pay the debts we honor
Though,
Still not making it on one income
To raise a family of "One point One"
This is the time we are living in
This is the time of my life

It's Time for Me to Go

Yesterday,
I stood tall
In front of all
Life's obstacles and challenges,
My friend
Today,
I stand
In front of you,
Weak and humbled
Short of words
To express my fears and my pain
I am afraid to say
My life on earth,
Has been cut short
And "It's Time for Me to Go"
I'm certain,
I'm leaving
I'm uncertain,
Where I'm going
It took 9 months
To prepare me
To be born in this world
I am afraid to say
There isn't enough time
In the universe
To prepare me
Out of this place
I am traveling on a journey
It's called the "Journey of Death"
What an ugly name for a journey
I won't be taking my bike or my pipe
I won't be taking any food or drinks

I won't be taking
Anything or anyone with me
I won't be doing the traveling
My soul will be traveling for me
I hope,
I've prepared my soul,
For this journey
God have mercy on my soul,
If I haven't done enough
And my friend
Please, forgive me
If I've been
Too short with you
Remember me
I'll always remember you
Speak of my name
I will always hear you
Pray for me
Your prayer will be
My soul's companion
But, have no fear
And, shed no tear
Soon,
All of my fears will be gone
And, I'll be
Re-born in another universe

Dawn

A Moment of Clarity	95
Amending the Past	98
A Runaway Child	101
I Believe in You	103
Finding the Answers	107
I Know You	111
Life's Mysterious Encounters	114
Hope	118

A Moment of Clarity

On a Monday morning
Early in June
Sitting all alone
In my room
Gazing at the walls
Listening to the tones
Sounds playing in my head
Nothing was in tune

Strange faces
Shady places
And the full moon
It was coming up
On three days, soon
Since I'd been up
Partying with my goons

They all left me behind
With no party favors or booze
Dude, I was so doomed
If you know what I mean

Searching for something
To lift me out of this gloom
Found a couple of hits
Still resonating in a spoon
As I lit up and inhaled
That smoky plume
Felt it rushing
Through my lungs and my head
Like a "Sonic Boom"
Ahhhhh, where is my dealer

Stoner "B-Cool"
He's getting me some supplies
By mid-afternoon

Rushing to place a call
For a delivery
Tripping over my dog XTC
Forgetting to call
My girl Tiffany
And totally blowing off
Band practice with my buddies

All upset in a tizzy
Calling me
Many names in profanity
You couldn't find
In the dictionary
So I shut them all out
In a hurry
And started my own party
Of self pity
As I began panicking
And breathing heavy
Falling deeper and deeper
In my misery
Thinking,
What's becoming
Of my reality?
And what got me into
This calamity
Should I be calling
My dealer for remedy
Or someone else
To help me

Save my sanity
As I paused for
"A Moment of Clarity"
Wondering,
What would become
Of my odyssey
A dope head
Marked on my tombstone
Or
A healer
To the youth I've known
Surrender it all
To the drugs roping me my soul
Or, get my free will back
And claim my own
As I paused for
"A Moment of Clarity"

Amending the Past

Days of our lives
Passing us by
In a blink of an eye
Leaving us behind
Singing songs
Of hearts felt wounds
Tugging along
Memories
Of too many wrongs

Grew up alone
In haunted homes
Along the streets
Of broken dreams

Resenting those years
Of drama and fear
Of our early
Childhood years

Robbing us blind
Molding us bad
Angry and mad
Cynically proud
Calling it loud
As we sat
By the curbside
Drinking wine
Killing time
Awaiting someone
Calling our names
To board the train

Going on
A roller coaster ride
Through the "Journey of Life"
Crossing many time zones
Lives of our own
Going up and down
Through sharp turns
And rough terrains
Arriving on time
To a dead end, my friend

Wondering
What, the hell, was that all about
It's not what we had in mind
Nor what we had planned
Arguing and debating
Who, where, what and why
As if, it matters
How much we whine
Wishing,
For the time to rewind
To bring us the past alive
To help us understand
How the present we had
Became the past we have
Without being summoned
For us to decide
On the future
Of our lives

Taking, a stance
Wanting to enhance
Our lives in a glance
Daydreaming of a chance

In "Amending the Past"
In trance,
Till,
We heard the sound
Of a chanting voice
Echoing loud
Dictating words
Simple and profound
Saying,
To the crowds

Let it be known
Your destiny,
Has been mapped,
By the work,
Of your hand
The future,
Shall unfold,
As it's empowered
And told
By the willpower
Of your word

You are in command
All awaiting you to decide
Go ahead and take the lead
Into the future,
You most desire and need

To be the same,
Just do the same
To have it different,
Just do it different
It's, just,
As simple
As that

A Runaway Child

Run, Run, Runaway
Run from the dark memories of yesterday
Run from the ugly realities of today
Run from the loneliness of each day
Run to the streets for a sanctuary
Run to the Street Kids for a family
Run from the verbal insults
Run from the sexual assaults
Run from the physical onslaught
Run from the haunting doubts
And the dreadful thoughts

Wondering
How long this shit is going to last
Is this the way
It's supposed to be?
Or is it just me?
To be
"A Runaway Child"
Traveling as a Nomad
Across the Motherland
Seeking the world outside
For a helping hand

Only to be
Disappointed and sad
Discouraged and mad
Broken down to the ground
As I laid down and cried
Resigned
No way out
Confined

Till,
I heard the sound
Calling me
To get up
And
To take a stand
To dig deep inside
My heart and my mind

As I realized
It's I
Who needs to decide
When
To turn my life around
Then,
I shall find
My own
Peace-Of-Mind

I Believe in You

Have you been living
The life you've been given
Or, have you given up
On the life you're living

Are you still dwelling
On the past
And for how long
Will you be planning
To do just that

Have you given up
On your dreams
To your anxiety,
Doubts and fear

Is it too much
To ask of you and bother
Or is it
Politically incorrect
And improper

Calling me
Normal or up-normal
Conservative or Liberal
A sinner or a winner
It doesn't really matter

Cause, it's you
Sisters and Brothers
Who I'm
Talking about

Why, do I see you
Doubting your ability
Trusting your liability
Dodging the possibilities
Ignoring the opportunities
Hesitant and reluctant
Trapped in and uncertain
Of what you're all about
Aren't you tough enough
You, you're yourself,
Aren't You
So, what're you afraid of
Why you so scared

Why wouldn't you try
Lifting your head up high
In reaching out to the stars
Brightly illuminating the skies
You may end happy
For, just, giving it a try

You know
You are as hopeful as you believe
And as hopeless as you want to be
You are
As powerful as I see
And powerless
As you claim to be

What's holding you back?
Is it the fear
Of what you don't see?
Or, is it the lack of belief
On your part to achieve?

Or, could it be
The lack of deed
On your part to succeed?

Many born
Quickly grown
Putting their lives on hold
Waiting to be told
Till they became too old
While watching
Their dreams erode
Robbed blind
Of solid gold
Dreams and hopes
Their choice
Their voice
They gave up too soon
Surrendering quitters
Blaming others
As if, they didn't know any better

All of the B.S. and talk
Won't change
A damn thing of your past

I'm not interested
In hearing your story
I'm only here
To see your glory

Don't shut me out
Cause you don't like
What I am talking about

Why won't you be
The bad-ass driver

Driving your own vehicle
To a brighter future

Why won't you be
The kick-ass fighter
Fighting for
Your own survival

Why won't you be
The hard-ass boss
Bossing yourself
Out of any chaos

Why won't you be
The a gangster
Ganging up
On your disaster

To be a winner
You've got to run
With the winners
To be a loser
You don't need me
To give you a clue
For an answer

Go ahead
Walk your talk
Only then
You shall find out
What you are all about

I believe in you
Do you believe in you?

Finding the Answers

My friend
Tough times
Come around
At utmost
Inopportune time
Determined
To defy
What you're
All about

Leaving you behind
Wondering
How much shit could pile up
How fast
And for how long it could last
Testing your patience
Defying your resilience
Bringing you grief
Beyond belief
Pushing,
Your hot buttons
Sending you
Flying through the roof
Singing the blues
Then,
Knocking you down
Till you drown
On your 7 and crown

Though,
Still, not amused,
Running, confused

And seeking refuge
From everyone
Not wanting
Anyone
To clutter
Your thoughts
Nor bog you down
In shock,
Denying it
In doubt,
Fighting it
Thinking and debating
Of all the things
Taking place in your life
Till you begin
Hearing
An inner voice
Coming from within
It's your voice
It's your choice
It's the answer
To the encounter
You were having
Discovering it,
By, reaching within
Rather than
Reaching out

At other times
You shall remain
Far from reaching
Any viable answer
Burdened beyond
Your comprehension
Outside the realm
Of your thinking

Unable to fathom
The meaning of
"The light at the end of the tunnel"

Such encounters
Descend on us
To reach out further
In search of
The clues
Given in the cues
Through countless
Living creatures
And
Surrounding features

A youthful heart
Of an aging man
An old soul
Of a young girl
A gaze
At a shimmering star
Brightly illuminating the skies
Or a pair of birds
Mating on the fly
A cry of vulnerability
A prayer for humility

Ask questions
And just listen
No need to
Agree or disagree
Accept or reject
Act or react

Free your intuitions
Rid yourself
Of all inhibitions
Allow your senses to be
Receptors
Of magical powers
Helping you discover
The answers
To the encounters
You were having
And
At utmost
Opportune time
By
Reaching out
Rather than
Reaching within

I Know You

I know you
I am you
I am merely,
An image of you
I've lived in your shadow
I've shared your sorrow
I am the true voice,
You hear
I am the cure,
Helping you heal
I am your guide
I am at your side
I am the lightning rod
Helping you stand
Stead fast to the sod

I'm wondering, now
Why do I see you
Copping out
Vowing
In letting go
Of life
Of my life
Of your life
Surrendering
Your existence
Without resistance
Oblivious
To what it's all about
Crying out loud
You wanted a new start
Now, that, it's here

You want it to disappear
Don't you get it?
To each of your setbacks
There is a treasure,
Awaiting your comeback
Each conquest you make
Determines
What awaits you next
After your final rest
All alone
On your own
No one around
Other than you
My Sister
You, too,
My Brother

I am your conscience
I am conspicuous
Find me or not
I won't rest
Till you are
At your best
Have no doubt
What I am about
No need to figure me out
Yesterday, forever disappeared
Tomorrow, may never appear
But today, you are here
What you do today
You shall reap tomorrow
Regardless
If you are dead or alive

Go ahead and take a chance
On something, otherwise
You would never have
Breathe deep
Let the blood flow to your heart
Let your mind do its miraculous art
Let your eyes help you hear
Let your ears help you see
Live your life and be alive
Go on living
Don't be denying
Yourself
Any moment of it

Thinking
You have an eternity to live
Think, again

Life's Mysterious Encounters

In your pursuit of
Your basic needs
Or
Your future grand dreams

Life's mysterious encounters
Descend on us
Bringing
Treasures to discover
Or
Nightmares to uncover

Such encounters
May be incidents
But they are
Hardly accidents

Do not brush them off
Deny them
Nor, write them off

Take the time to vent
As, you reminisce each event

Let your emotions go
Give yourself
Some time to grow

Shed your tears
Moreover,
Confront your fears

Speak of your hardship
To the ones
Honoring your friendship

Let people know
Where you stand
Even if they were to think
You've gone mad

You won't make everyone glad
No matter
How many times you try

Your loved ones will be proud,
Knowing that
You've done your best
Any time
You were put through the test

Humble yourself
To the ground
It takes a lot of courage
To do just that

Patience is a virtue
Most of us,
Don't have
Making us,
Look bad
Reacting mad
Out of the fear
Residing in our hearts
From the memories
Of our past
Toward many things
We, still, don't understand

Help someone in need
An act of a good dead
Pays us back
In lighting speed

Cherish each moment
In time
Before, you know it,
Soon, it'll be gone

Don't go into remission
Till someone
Grants you permission
To go on living
The life
You've been given

Everyone can be right
About something
If we just, try listening

Do not waste too much time
Fighting your friends or love ones
'Cause,
Neither one
Will help you
Get anything done
Besides,
It's not much fun

Learn as much as you can
About yourself
Before you go on
Changing everyone else

Thinking inside the box
Is rarely done
So thinking prematurely
Outside of it
Is just dump

Keep in mind
Regardless, if such encounters
Were Karma getting you back
Or new lessons of life to add
Just consider them
As if they were hurdles
On another mountain climb
Helping you ascend
To new heights
Knowing well
It only gets harder
As you, go up higher
To the top

Life is an adventure
For anyone
Who wouldn't surrender

You only have
One round trip
To mother earth
So might as will
Make it all it is worth

Hope

You spoke of Hope, in dismay
Lots of pain, you don't care
Trials and tribulations, not fair
Endless drama
Never ending nightmares
In despair
Gasping for air

The "Past," was a bear
More than,
You could handle, I swear
The "Future" is a blur
Opportunities are rare
Living my life
But, going nowhere
What is there for me to acquire
It's just a waste of time," you utter
Why shouldn't I be angry and bitter
Toward the life I hate
My "Karma" and "Fate"

Karma?
Trauma?
Master of drama
I've got you covered
Not a devil's advocate
Nor, a cynic
Can win you over
Why wouldn't you let go
Of all the misery and woe
To give yourself
Some time to grow

Don't you know
Barren grounds,
Begin breathing,
After a long rainy season
Angry volcanoes,
Calm down,
After they've been screaming,
Hot lava and burning
The darkest of all eerie nights,
Start leaving for the twilight,
By the breaking dawn of each morning

Why wouldn't you embrace Hope
It just might be the answer
To all your prayers

Hope does honor
Those folks who face the fact
Take responsibility for their act
Moreover,
Rarely blame the past
For any fault of their own

Hope does honor
Those who aren't quitters
Even if their lives get ten times tougher

Hope does honor
Those who won't abandon
Their future dreams no matter
How tough or unreal

Hope does honor
Those who are eager

To venture out and discover
What life may have to offer
Regardless of age or gender
Religion or skin color
A child crawling few feet
Or learning how to eat
A teenager taking a new class
Or writing a novel of romance
An adult picking up a new language to speak
Or climbing roof tops and mounts' peaks

Hope does honor
Those trusting it to deliver
On its promise no matter
Descending upon your shoulder
Like an Angel undiscovered
Bringing you surreal magic and power
Lasting you forever
Affirmed by your daughter
As she whispers
"Your are my best friend, Mother"

Affirmed by friends letters
Promising to be at your side, no matter

Do your best
Embrace "Hope" to your chest
Then, leave to God the rest

Bright Light

Future Dreams 123
Sweet 16.. 125
A Smile 128
Till death, do us apart.. 132
Friends of a Rare Breed.. 135
Self-Worth 137
Tough Times for Old Souls 142
Diamonds in the Rough.. 145

Future Dreams

"I have a dream "
The words
Of
A
"King"
Calling out
To
Bring
A
Nation
To
Sing
"Let Freedom Ring"
For
Women and Men
And
For all children

Determined
To
Make it happen

Willing
To
Sacrifice everything

Ended up giving
His
Life and living
For
A
Noble Mission

Surreal

A gleam in a dream
A vision of a scene
A dire need to lead
On
A mission to proceed

Planned.....................to deliver
Constructed...........in pleasure
Maintained..................forever
Illuminated..... with willpower
Commissioned........to redeem
Future ....dreams

Tomorrow's scene
Merely
A mirror reflecting
Today's deeds
In pursuit of
Yesterday's Dreams

If it is meant to be, it will be
Nothing ventured, nothing gained

Sweet 16

A High School queen
A teen idol
Living her dreams
A runway model
To be seen
On the cover of
Teens magazine

Flying out
To the scenes
Hoping
For a lead
Helping her
Appear
On the "Big Screen"

Serene
Tall and lean
Wearing sexy tight jeans
By Ralph Lauren

With a tank top
Revealing
Her crevices and ravines
Matching
The color of her skin
By Donna Karan

With eye liner and shadows
In shades of green
From New York's
Maybelline

Gucci Shades
Prada Purse
Chanel Scent
Dollars spent
Stopping in between
For "Starbucks" caffeine

It's just
A part of the routine
In today's teen

Times have changed
For a "Sweet 16"
While coming of age
As she'd be dreaming
Of her "Charming Prince"
Holding out and waiting
For that first kiss

Getting dressed up
And excited
For her formal
Dinner date
Promising Mommy and Daddy
She won't be out too late

While attending to practice
For her Driver's license
As the sign of marking
Her coming of age

Today's "Sweet 16"
May appear to be
A material girl

Hardened
And unreal
From all
She had seen

Rest assured
Her heart is pure
Her soul will endure
She is only becoming
A stronger
Young Woman,
And, Mature

Go ahead sing a song
Knowing well
Life won't last too long

Leave your past behind
It won't much add
To the life you still have

Free your mind
From all that is pinning you down
Have fun
No need to run
Yourself ragged to the ground

Don't give your bouts
Lots of thought
Soon, you'll forget
What they were about

Say, pardon me
Excuse me
Or any other
Frecking word you want
But, don't wait
For far too long
Till you find
The special ones
In your life
Just passed away
Before you could say
Goodbye to them

Live your life
Be alive
Love many
Including your enemies
Cause
There won't be any
After we die

Free your heart
From hate and anger
Cause, it'll cost you
Hanging on them much longer

These words
Come your way
Do not pretend
You cannot hear
Or ignore them for years
Go ahead and spread the cheers

Till death, do us apart

She wondered
If she'd ever meet Mr. Right
He doubted
If he'd ever tie the knot

Till, one night
Late last summer
As they were meeting
Their friends for diner
And ended up
Setting together
Unable to keep their eyes
Off each other
Sending sparks
Flying and igniting
Flames of passion
In their hearts
Serendipity at its might
Love at first sight
Hesitant and frightened
Euphoric, and excited
Not wanting to be apart
As they started going out
On lots of walks and talks
Kissing and making out

As if, they knew
They were meant for each other

What a sight
Seeing her
Dressed up

Beautifully in white
A shimmering star
Exquisitely and bright
Illuminating
Her lover's way to her heart
As her trembling lips
Nervously, recite
"I'll be your wedded wife…
… till death do us part"
Droplets of tears
Running down her cheeks
Wondering,
If she'd make him happy

As he stood there,
Tensed up nervously
Holding her hand
Firmly tight
Assuring her
They'll be alright
Despite,
His fear and anxiety
A gentleman,
Handsomely
Dressed smart
Appearing as thee
"Knight in Shining Armor"
Whispering to her comfort
Blowing her a kiss with a smile
While gazing at her lips
And lost in her eyes

Asking her
If she'd accept him to be
Her wedded husband

Promising,
To love her for the rest of time
To shield her from any harm
To fulfill her dreams
And to be her partner for life

She accepted him with a kiss
As they were pronounced
"Husband and Wife"

A celebration of being in love
And a promise to be the nurturer of love
A celebration of being a soul mate
And a promise to be a true mate of the soul
A celebration of being faithful
And a promise to be always faithful
A celebration of being a friend
And a promise to be each other's best friend

Regardless
Of the price to pay
Or the sacrifice to make

Love is surreal
Friendship is real
Respect and trust each other
If you want the marriage,
To last forever
No one is perfect,
So, help each other be
Patience is power
Forgiveness is beyond all
And don't forget
To talk to each other

Friends of a Rare Breed

Someone.
You hardly knew
Whom,
You'd never call unto
At times
You were going through
Life's lessons
Of "Drama and Blues"

As problems,
Began to loom
And, people,
Began to detour
Leaving you behind
Drowning in a slough
Alone, on your own
Restless,
Without a clue
Lost,
And confused
Praying
To endure
Those moments
Of gloom

Suddenly, appear
Bright lights and pure
Of old souls and mature
Coming
For the rescue
Honoring you
For being true
To all those whom you knew

In today's
Chaos and greed
And at times
Of desperate need
Only a few
Who'll transcend
To offer and lend
A helping a hand
Till you get your feet
Back on the ground

Who'll be at your side
Till you heal and mend

Who'll be your guide
Through life's bends
And dead ends

Honor them indeed
For being
True
"Friends of a Rare Breed"

Self-Worth

Descending on earth
A miraculous birth
An embryo loom
Cohabiting in a womb
Sustained in warmth
Nurtured for growth
Born into the world
Breathing on your own
A Mystical Myth
In that first breath
A sign of life
And being alive
Needing attention
Parental affection
Thriving on
Food for nutrition
Learning for living
Friends and lovers
Wealth in dollars
Yearning for a home
A family of your own
Groomed and refined
For thee
Test of your life
Defying you
To find yourself
Daring you
To define your self-worth
Bringing you grief
Beyond belief
Pushing you
To the edge

Leaving you behind,
Hanging,
On a thread
Off,
A lousy ledge
Till you become
Broken,
Into ruins

Emptiness takes place
Sadness fills the space
Self-destruct imposed
Self-respect ignored
Continuing to reason
Refusing to accept
Something is missing
Valuing life and living
In people and material things
Vulnerable to all
Someone
Breaking your heart
Mounting
Debts out of sight
Dying
Friend or a child
Or losing
Your cat or dog
Discovering
In their disappearing
You've got nothing
In shock, still denying
Not fazed by it
Still resisting
Refusing to acknowledge

Something else had been missing
Hanging on nothing
Searching for something
Not knowing
What you were looking for
Exhausted and run down
Beat as I laid down
With a needle
In my arm
Calm
Feeling
No harm
Painless
Weightless
Space less
No sound
Two seconds
Maybe less
Before
I was gone
Out cold
Eyes closed
Skin frozen
Stopped breathing
Slowly dying
Not knowing why
I didn't try
To stay alive
Or, just say
Good-bye
That night
Uncertain

"I was asleep,"
"Wasn't I?"

Please, tell me
Am I alright
I, did!
What?
I,
Died!
For God's sake
Why?

How long,
Was I gone
Before, I started
To breath on my own

Opening my eyes
To see her smile
What a saving grace
Seeing her face
An Angel,
From outer space
Brought me back my soul
Signaling me with her hand
While counting the beats
Of my heart
Telling me
She was so glad
I'm still around

As a sigh of relief
Filled the space
Paramedics,
Fire Fighters,
And the Police
Asking them

For forgiveness, please
For disrupting their lives
And bringing them fear
Just hours
Before
The early morning
Sunrise
While daydreaming
Of the tears
Of my Mother's
Saddened weary eyes

My self-worth,
Had been missing
Getting it back,
Is my blessing

It's time
For me
To begin
Living
The life
I've been given

And pursue
My soul's
Mission
After
It came back
From it's,
Remission

Tough Times for Old Souls

What is the essence of a Soul?
If I can't identify with it at all
How could it be so old?
If I couldn't recall
My past existence at all
How can I be a Believer
Of a Higher Power?
As I watch, people die and suffer
In the name of the Father
Is it a wonder?
Or just a blunder

What is the propose of it all
Celebrating its arrival
Mourning its departure
Landing into this world
Each time a baby is born
Coming into our lives
Bringing with it a fetus to life
All born at an infancy stage
Departing without regards to age
Is it a wonder?
Or just a blunder

Memories fade away
Help us
Cope each day
Time mysteriously disappears
Faster and faster each year
Good and bad intertwine
Just like
Daylight and night, entwine

Life is not in our hand
Living is up to us to decide
Is it a wonder?
Or just a blunder

Happiness is attained
Only after overcoming
Agony and pain
Sounds insane
For a birthing mother
Needing to suffer
Each time
She delivers
Before she could attain
Any joy or pleasure
Ordained
No Pain, No Gain
Is it a wonder?
Or just a blunder

Body, Mind and Soul
Embodied together in uniform
Living societal norms
Seeking answers on its own
Wondering how it all works
Is it all up to the journey our soul takes?
Or is it about the stops we make?
As we often, wonder
Or is it just a blunder

Life's lessons not to be ignored
From the disasters you survived
To the ones that haven't arrived
Grieve each dark moment you had

Regardless how much comfort you have
Rest assured
Each time you endure
You become more mature
Your soul gets more pure
Pray and believe in the higher power
Even if you doubt its existence forever
You may wonder
But it's not a blunder

Diamonds in the Rough

Never doubt your purity
And surrender it to the roughness
Of your childhood memories

Your purity was formed
At your birth by your loving Mother
Your impurity was adulterated
Over time by many others

Do not surrender
To the doubts you may have
Your precious soul
Will endure the hardship you had

It's your choice to shine, again
Or vanish in the dark clouds in vain
Don't close your mind or heart
And relinquish your soul to vanish in the dark

Your purity will endure
The dark memories of yesterday
And your scratches and roughness
Will fade away

It is time to awaken your spirit and heart
For my presence in your life
It's just to show you the start

Rise above the treasures
And ugly events of your past
For nothing on earth
Shall ever last

Let go of the agony, pain
And unhealthy doubts
To give room for hope and beauty
Occupy your thoughts

Stop running away and hiding
From life's endeavors
And begin the healing, living
And attending to the others

For the precious diamond within you
Has healing powers
Passed onto you
By your Loving Mother

NASH HASAN came from the Middle East to the United States in 1978 at the age of 18 to attend college in Gainesville, Texas. He moved to Oregon in 1979, and earned his B.S. Structural Eng degree in 1982 and his MBA Eng Management degree in 1986.

Mr. Hasan spent 23 years in Construction and Facility Management, 10 years conducting Management and Leadership training seminars, 12 years serving on boards of various non-profit professional organizations, and a 1-year term as a Director on the Board of Directors of IFMA - Global. He resigned his careers in October 2006 to dedicate his time and energy fully toward writing this book.

Nash attributes much of his success to the compassion and the support he received from his family and friends in the Middle East, Texas, and Oregon.